SUMMER OF SUSPENSE

For Jemma, Nicholas, Harry and Georgina

1986 Cornhill Test Series
England v India and New Zealand

SUMMER OF SUSPENSE

PATRICK EAGAR

with commentary by Alan Ross

PARTRIDGE PRESS

Photographs © 1986 by Patrick Eagar
Text copyright © 1986 by Alan Ross

Published in Great Britain by
Partridge Press
Maxwelton House
Boltro Road
Haywards Heath
West Sussex

(Partridge Press is an imprint of
Transworld Publishers Limited
61/63 Uxbridge Road
London W5 5SA)

Designed by Jo Laws
Photographic prints by Jan Traylen

Printed in Great Britain by
BAS Printers Limited
Over Wallop
Hampshire

1–85225–019–4

Contents

Introduction

The summer of 1986 was, for most of England's cricketers, as gloomy an experience as the winter had been. Shaken up and humiliated in the Caribbean, the batsmen at least must have had expectations of salvaging respect against the milder attacks of India and New Zealand. Until the very last of the six Tests at the Oval they failed signally to do so, though there were isolated moments of splendour from Gooch, Gower and Gatting, the last two signing off in late August with the most dashing batting of the summer.

The England bowling rarely rose above the nondescript. Edmonds and Emburey as usual wheeled away steadily but they bowled a lot of overs for their wickets and by crowding the batsmen allowed themselves no margin for error and little scope for variations of flight. None of the quicker bowlers impressed. Radford seemed out of his class, Thomas was erratic and expensive, and Small, after a promising start, looked distressingly plain at the Oval. Dilley, smoother in approach and delivery than in his earlier days, was just about the best of them. By the end of the summer, Gooch having declined to go to Australia, England had not even half an opening pair of batsmen and no settled opening attack.

These were domestic problems, of little concern to the Indians and New Zealanders, both of whom deservedly took their respective Cornhill Test series as well as the Texaco trophies.

India, for whom Vengsarkar as a batsman had a brilliant June, confounded England with medium paced bowling that held admirably to line and length. Their batsmen were more technically correct and played straighter than England's did and whenever runs were needed someone usually produced them.

The New Zealanders, eagerly led by Jeremy Coney, looked the better organised and more determined of the two sides. They depended, inevitably, on Hadlee's bowling to get them into dominating positions but they were far from a one-man band. Martin Crowe, Bracewell and Wright all made hundreds and Coney, with a top score of 51, still managed to average 44. Gray proved a useful all-rounder and both Hadlee and Edgar had their moments as batsmen.

It was, nevertheless, the consistently wonderful fast-medium bowling of Richard Hadlee that gave New Zealand, already victorious over Australia at home and away in the last year, their first series in England. Master of all the arts, of the ball that cuts back or leaves the bat, of the occasional bouncer, Hadlee made every England batsman wary and uncomfortable. He bowled long spells and never flagged. He took more than double the wickets of any other bowler in either side and the variations of his skill were absorbing to watch. It had not been ever thus. A decade earlier he had bowled off a run twice as long and half as effectively.

If neither the ill-starred venture to the Caribbean nor either of the two Test series of the summer threw up any likely stars of the future for England, there were possibilities in the younger generation. The outstanding batsman among them was certainly Graeme Hick, the powerfully built Zimbabwean who cannot qualify for England for another five years, but there were others of more than passing interest: J. J. Whitaker of Leicestershire, R. J. Bailey of Northamptonshire, A. A. Metcalfe of Yorkshire, each of whom, though in their first-class infancy look England batsmen of the near future. Hick is still only 20, Whitaker 24, Bailey 22, Metcalfe 22. Among all-rounders the 20-year-old Phillip De Freitas, Dominican-born and in his second season with Leicestershire, made strides as a lively bowler who can bat more than a bit.

English bowling in general remained at a low ebb. Of the top ten in the averages on September 1st, only two were qualified to play for England: J. H. Childs, a 35 year-old slow left arm bowler discarded by Gloucestershire and now with Essex, and Jack Simmons, the 45 year-old Lancashire offspinner. This may say something for them but not much for the others.

Of the next dozen or so only Jarvis, aged 20 and a fast-medium bowler now picking up wickets regularly for Yorkshire, and Foster, in and out of the England side but still only 24, mean much in a Test match context. The most successful spinner, after Childs and Simmons, was Gifford, aged 46. Slow bowlers, we know, take time to mature, but this was ridiculous.

As the summer began with extensive publicity given to Botham's misdemeanours, so it ended with equal coverage of Somerset's decision not to re-engage Garner and Richards, and Botham's declaration that if they went he would go, too. Whether this gesture of solidarity is carried out or not, he himself enlivened August with a battery of sixes. A season of suspense and suspension ended with little resolved.

First Test

LORD'S · 5–10 June

India came to Lord's in June for the Cornhill Test with little cricket behind them. They had won the Texaco Trophy, on a faster overall scoring rate, both sides winning a match each, but otherwise May had been a month of distractions: wet, blustery conditions, the American bombing of Libya from British bases, the prolonged deliberations over Botham.

Cricket in such circumstances takes a back seat. The weather remained wintry, more Simla than Calcutta. England got off to a reasonable start, Robinson, away from his West Indian tormentors, batting in the relaxed fashion he had demonstrated in India and against the Australians. But with the fall of his wicket at 66 the first of many of the match collapses set in. Within the space of six runs Sharma, making haste off the pitch, removed Gower, Gatting and Lamb. Gooch, taking an unusual amount of time over his runs, reached a responsible hundred and England recovered to 245 for 4 before he was out, also to Sharma.

Gooch and Pringle had put on 147 together, but thereafter no-one had much to offer.

India began fluently, Amarnath, off-driving and pulling racing to his fifty. The spinners slowed things down but Azharuddin, as usual, was quickly into his stride and with Vengsarkar installed at the other end India at one stage were 230 for 3.

Once Azharuddin was out, brilliantly caught and bowled by Dilley, the innings fell away. Only some stout resistance by the wicket-keeper, More, enabled Vengsarkar to reach an increasingly becoming hundred, his third Test hundred at Lord's. India eventually acquired a fragile lead of 47.

It turned out to be crucial. On a sunless fourth day the Indian medium paced bowlers got the ball to move about, reducing England to 35 for 3. Gatting and Lamb put on 73 but once they were out the batting became increasingly desultory and strokeless. Maninder polished off the tail, taking 3 for 9 in 20 overs.

India had the whole of the last day to make 134. They lost 20 minutes at the start and for a while the weather was as much a cause of anxiety as the England attack, at various times without both Dilley and Emburey. Wickets fell at regular intervals 10, 31, 76, 78, 110, but Kapil Dev and Shastri were having no nonsense. Shastri cracked Edmonds for three fours in an over and then Kapil Dev heaved him into the Grandstand for six. After the match Gower was relieved of the England captaincy, Gatting being put in charge for the two remaining Tests against India.

ENGLAND v. INDIA—First Test

Toss: India

ENGLAND: First Innings

G. A. Gooch, b Sharma	114
R. T. Robinson, c Azharuddin, b Maninder	35
*D. I. Gower, c More, b Sharma	18
M. W. Gatting, b Sharma	0
A. J. Lamb, c Srikkanth, b Sharma	6
D. R. Pringle, b Binny	63
J. E. Emburey, c Amarnath, b Kapil Dev	7
†P. R. Downton, lbw b Sharma	5
R. M. Ellison, c Kapil Dev, b Binny	12
G. R. Dilley, c More, b Binny	4
P. H. Edmonds, not out	7
Extras (lb 15, w 1, nb 7)	23

TOTAL 294

Fall of Wickets: 1-66, 2-92, 3-92, 4-98, 5-245, 6-264, 7-269, 8-271, 9-287.

Bowling: Kapil Dev 31-8-67-1; Binny 18.2-4-55-3; Skarma 32-10-64-5; Maninder 30-15-45-1; Amarnath 7-1-18-0; Shastri 10-3-30-0.

ENGLAND: Second Innings

G. A. Gooch, lbw b Kapil Dev	8
R. T. Robinson, c Amarnath, b Kapil Dev	11
*D. I. Gower, lbw b Kapil Dev	8
M. W. Gatting, b Sharma	40
A. J. Lamb, c More, b Shastri	39
D. R. Pringle, c More, b Kapil Dev	6
†P. R. Downton, c Shastri, b Maninder	29
†R. M. Ellison, c More, b Binny	19
J. E. Emburey, c and b Maninder	1
G. R. Dilley, not out	2
P. H. Edmonds, c Binny, b Maninder	7
Extras (lb 6, w 1, nb 3)	10

TOTAL 180

Fall of Wickets: 1-18, 2-23, 3-35, 4-108, 5-113, 6-121, 7-164, 8-170, 9-170.

Bowling: Kapil Dev 22-7-52-4; Sharma 17-4-48-1; Binny 15-3-44-1; Shastri 20-8-21-1; Maninder 20.4-12-9-3; Amarnath 2-2-0-0.

INDIA: First Innings

S. M. Gavaskar, c Emburey, b Dilley	34
K. Srikkanth, c Gatting, b Dilley	20
M. Amarnath, c Pringle, b Edmonds	69
D. B. Vengsarkar, not out	126
M. Azharuddin, c and b Dilley	33
R. J. Shastri, c Edmonds, b Dilley	1
R. M. H. Binny, lbw b Pringle	9
*Kapil Dev, c Lamb, b Ellison	1
C. Sharma, b Pringle	2
†K. S. More, lbw b Pringle	25
Maninder Singh, c Lamb, b Emburey	6
Extras (lb 5, w 1, nb 9)	15

TOTAL 341

Fall of Wickets: 1-31, 2-90, 3-161, 4-232, 5-238, 6-252, 7-253, 8-264, 9-303.

Bowling: Dilley 34-7-146-4; Ellison 29-11-63-1; Emburey 27-13-28-1; Edmonds 22-7-41-1; Pringle 25-7-58-3.

INDIA: Second Innings

S. M. Gavaskar, c Downton, b Dilley	22
K. Srikkanth, c Gooch, b Dilley	0
M. Amarnath, lbw b Pringle	8
D. B. Vengsarkar, b Edmonds	33
M. Azharuddin, run out	14
R. J. Shastri, not out	20
*Kapil Dev, not out	23
Extras (lb 9, b 1, w 1, nb 5)	16

TOTAL (5 wkts) 136

Fall of Wickets: 1-10, 2-31, 3-76, 4-78, 5-110.

Bowling: Dilley 10-3-28-2; Ellison 6-0-17-0; Pringle 15-5-30-1; Edmonds 11-2-51-1.

Umpires: K. E. Palmer and D. R. Shepherd.

INDIA won by 5 wickets.

Graham Gooch, after a moody and troubled winter in the Caribbean, returned to Test cricket with a century. For all the menace of the black bristles below the flaps of his helmet this was not one of his more dismissive innings; rather a patient re-adjustment to circumstances and conditions.

With Gower at the end of a rope, Gatting was next in line. He could have done with runs here, on his home ground, but the bustling Sharma, short of stature but skiddy off the pitch, quickly knocked his off-stump out. Sharma finished with 5-64.

Lamb lasted only a few balls more than Gatting, Srikkanth picking him up at forward short leg off Sharma. It was no picnic for Lamb but for Kapil Dev, the bowler and the wicket-keeper the removal of three top-line batsmen within the space of a few minutes justifies a jig of delight.

BELOW Pringle, the obvious replacement for Botham, batted for four and a half hours and with Gooch took England from 98–4 to 245–5. No-one could complain about Pringle's performance in this match but whether batting or bowling he rarely seems able to impose himself quite enough to alter the course of a match.

LEFT David Gower leads England out but his hours as England's captain are numbered. He accepted his sacking as coolly and gracefully as he does everything, without attempting to disguise his regret.

RIGHT AND BELOW It was a momentous occasion for Dilip Vengsarkar whose third Test century at Lord's put him into the select company of Boycott, Compton, Hobbs, Hutton and John Edrich, the only overseas player among them. A frowning, edgy start to his innings gave way to a series of flicks off his legs, flashing cuts and skimming drives past the bowler. Left not out on 126 he had batted for four hours. His admirers advanced unceremoniously onto the pitch, not entirely to their hero's approval.

LEFT On perhaps the coldest day of the summer a girl sprinted half-naked out of the Grandstand and frolicked about on the pitch. What might have been an understandable effort to keep warm and entertain a crowd witnessing the fewest runs ever scored on a full day turned out disappointingly to be a publicity stunt. Edmonds sensibly avoids exposure to such depravity.

RIGHT Maninder Singh wearing, in the conditions, the most sensible headgear of all, bowled steadily to take 1 for 45 in 30 overs in England's first innings. He would have thought he was dreaming if he had foreseen figures of 3 for 9 in 20 overs in England's second innings on such a pitch.

BELOW Kieran More batted valiantly in support of Vengsarkar, in fact outscoring him in a partnership of 39 that helped India to turn the game. Behind the stumps, as here, he was prone to caper optimistically, his bionic ears picking up signals not apparent at the far end of the pitch.

LEFT Kapil Dev, moving the ball away and getting it to cut back, tore the heart out of England's second innings, removing Robinson, Gooch and Gower for one run. Gower never looked likely to settle in either innings, though he began here with two fine boundaries off Binny before falling lbw to Kapil Dev.

BELOW Amarnath, scraping the ball up at third slip, and his two colleagues appeal for a catch to make sure.

ABOVE LEFT Sunil Gavaskar, playing his last Test at Lord's made only modest contributions of 34 and 22, but even so his technique against the lifting ball and his poise were evident. He made only one fifty in the series but also only once scored less than 20. His hat was bought for a Buckingham Palace garden party.

ABOVE RIGHT There were still 18 runs to go but the idea of brown-wash was no illusion. The smiling faces tell their own story.

RIGHT David Gower awaits his fate, though it had already been decided. He had captained England 26 times, winning memorable series in India and at home against the Australians. To lose ten matches in a row against the vastly more powerful West Indians was possibly no disgrace in itself, but the manner of the defeats during the winter cost Gower his job. As he ruefully admitted he could not manufacture an aggressive demeanour, and if that was what was required he was plainly not the man for the job.

Second Test

HEADINGLEY · 19–23 June

India killed the 3-match Cornhill series stone dead, demolishing England by the huge margin of 279 runs. This was Gatting's first match as captain and England's seventh successive defeat. Gower, who injured a shoulder at Lord's, was unfit to play.

As a measure of the difference in batting consistency between the two sides, eleven of India's batsmen in their two innings scored 20 or more, as against three such scores by Englishmen, the highest being 32. Once again Dilip Vengsarkar was the outstanding batsman on view, scoring 61 and 102.

The match began in cool cloudy weather which became progressively colder. Conditions ought to have been ideal for England's bowlers on the opening day but none of them made the most of the possibilities, waywardness of both length and direction costing many runs. Only Kapil Dev, who was out first ball, lasted less than half an hour and seven Indian batsmen were in for over 80 minutes.

India, 235 for 8 at the end of the first day, were eventually all out for 272. This modest total acquired formidable proportions when England were hustled out for 102, having been 14 for 3, 41 for 5, and 71 for 8. Madan Lal, recruited at the last moment from the Central Lancashire League, and Binny both gave classic examples of accurate medium pace bowling, of the kind that has always thrived at Headingley in cloudy weather. By the end of a second day that saw 17 wickets fall England had reduced India to 70 for 5, but Vengsarkar found useful partners in Kapil Dev, Madan Lal and Binny, each making England's bowling seem increasingly plain and frivolous.

Set to make 408 England batted with depressing lack of spirit. Gooch was again quickly undone by Kapil Dev's bounce, Slack looked out of touch, and Lamb lost his wicket for the second time in the match to Binny for 10. Gatting was left high and dry with 31, Maninder Singh again wrapping up the tail. There was nothing to enthuse about in England's performance, except possibly a cool, composed innings of 32 by Athey and the efficient, unobtrusive wicket-keeping of French, who had replaced Downton.

ENGLAND v. INDIA—Second Test

Toss: India.

INDIA: First Innings

S. M. Gavaskar, c French, b Pringle	35
K. Srikkanth, c Emburey, b Pringle	31
R. J. Shastri, c Pringle, b Dilley	32
D. B. Vengsarkar, c French, b Lever	61
M. Azharuddin, lbw b Gooch	15
C. S. Pandit, c Emburey, b Pringle	23
*Kapil Dev, lbw b Lever	0
R. M. H. Binny, c Slack, b Emburey	6
Madan Lal, c Gooch, b Dilley	20
†K. S. More, not out	36
Maninder Singh, c Gooch, b Dilley	3
Extras (lb 5, nb 5)	10
TOTAL	**272**

Fall of Wickets: 1-64, 2-75, 3-128, 4-163, 5-203, 6-203, 7-211, 8-213, 9-267.

Bowling: Dilley 24.2-7-54-3; Lever 30-4-102-2; Pringle 27-6-47-3; Emburey 17-4-45-1; Gooch 6-0-19-1.

INDIA: Second Innings

S. M. Gavaskar, c French, b Lever	1
K. Srikkanth, b Dilley	8
R. J. Shastri, lbw b Lever	3
D. B. Vengsarkar, not out	102
M. Azharuddin, lbw b Lever	2
C. S. Pandit, b Pringle	17
†K. S. More, c Slack, b Pringle	16
*Kapil Dev, c Gatting, b Lever	31
Madan Lal, run out	22
R. M. H. Binney, lbw, b Pringle	26
Maninder Singh, c Gatting, b Pringle	1
Extras (lb 4 b 4)	8
TOTAL	**237**

Fall of Wickets: 1-9, 2-9, 3-29, 4-35, 5-70, 6-102, 7-137, 8-173, 9-233.

Bowling: Dilley 17-2-71-1; Lever 23-5-64-4; Pringle 22.3-6-73-4; Emburey 7-3-9-0; Gooch 7-2-12-0.

ENGLAND: First Innings

G. A. Gooch, c Binny, b Kapil Dev	8
W. N. Slack, b Madan Lal	0
C. L. Smith, b Madan Lal	6
A. J. Lamb, c Pandit, b Binny	10
*M. W. Gatting, c More, b Binny	13
C. W. J. Athey, c More, b Madan Lal	32
D. R. Pringle, c Srikkanth, b Binny	8
J. E. Emburey, c Kapil Dev, b Binny	0
†B. N. French, b Binny	8
G. R. Dilley, b Shastri	10
J. K. Lever, not out	0
Extras (lb 2, b 1, nb 4)	7
TOTAL	**102**

Fall of Wickets: 1-4, 2-14, 3-14, 4-38, 5-41, 6-63, 7-63, 8-71, 9-100.

Bowling: Kapil Dev 18-7-36-1; Madan Lal 11.1-3-18-3; Binny 13-1-40-5; Shastri 3-1-5-1.

ENGLAND: Second Innings

G. A. Gooch, c Srikkanth, b Kapil Dev	5
W. N. Slack, c Gavaskar, b Binny	19
C. L. Smith, c More, b Shastri	28
A. J. Lamb, c More, b Binny	10
*M. W. Gatting, not out	31
C. W. J. Athey, c More, b Maninder	8
J. K. Lever, c. More, b Maninder	0
D. R. Pringle, lbw b Maninder	1
J. E. Emburey, c Azharuddin, b Kapil Dev	1
†B. N. French, c Vengsarkar, b Maninder	5
G. R. Dilley, run out	2
Extras (lb 9, nb 2)	11
TOTAL	**128**

Bowling: Kapil Dev 19.2-7-24-2; Madan Lal 9.4-2-30-0; Binny 8-1-18-2; Maninder 16.3-6-26-4; Shastri 10-3-21-1.

Umpires: J. Birkenshaw and D. J. Constant.

INDIA won by 279 runs.

Mike Gatting, in charge for the first time, consults with Emburey. There was not much to blame Gatting himself for, but it must have been a disillusioning occasion, the crew ill-assorted, the winds cold.

ABOVE Gavaskar, sedately on view for 95 minutes, is caught behind the wicket off Pringle for 35.

BELOW Shastri wasted no time, hoisting Emburey for 4 before eventually falling to Dilley for 32.

RIGHT Lever took a lot of stick in his opening spell but he removed Vengsarkar and Kapil Dev with successive balls and took six wickets in the match for 166.

No wonder Maninder Singh, in the third of these pictures, looks bemused. He edged Dilley to Gooch at second slip, the ball bouncing out across first slip towards French who dived and just managed to scoop it up left-handed. Gooch flicked the ball neatly off his foot as it fell and then caught it.

ABOVE You might think this was Frank Tyson or at least Dennis Lillee bowling with the new ball, but in fact it is the modestly paced Roger Binny bowling to Athey with an oldish one.

RIGHT The ten packed together in a precarious row may or may not be cobbers of Mr Benaud but they seem to know a good commentator when they hear one. With the scoreboard showing 72 for 8 off 49 overs England need all the insurance they can get.

LEFT Madan Lal was not supposed to be a participant in this series but with Sharma unfit Kapil Dev summoned him over the Pennines from Ashton-under-Lyne. It was a shrewd move, for not only did Madan Lal, here seen getting one to nip back and bowl Smith between bat and pad, take 3 for 18 in England's shambles of a first innings, but he played two valuable innings of 20 and 22.

ABOVE Shastri is lbw to Lever for 3, the second of Lever's three early second innings wickets. Lever, recalled for this one match, justified his presence but watching England bat he must have wished he was back with Essex.

RIGHT Vengsarkar was occasionally beaten outside the off stump by Lever but otherwise, for three hours in the first innings and nearly five in the second, he never put a foot wrong. Beautifully still in stance Vengsarkar alternated the most correct of defensive strokes with crisp drives and cuts that brought him sixteen fours and one six. Here he pulls Pringle to square leg.

BELOW Smith batted an hour in
the second innings for 28 before
Shastri had him caught at the
wicket.

ABOVE RIGHT Athey is caught on
the legside off Maninder from
what must have been the barest
touch and England are 90 for 5.

BELOW RIGHT Pringle goes quietly
for the second time, lbw to
Maninder.

ABOVE Azharuddin, at third slip, catches Emburey off Kapil Dev. What looks like the start of a passing movement from a scrum-half ends with England on the way out.

BELOW Gatting looks back in anguish but Dilley is run out and it is all over, on a bare and bleak Monday morning. India bowled like professionals, England generally like club cricketers after a beery lunch. In batting technique there was no comparison between the two sides.

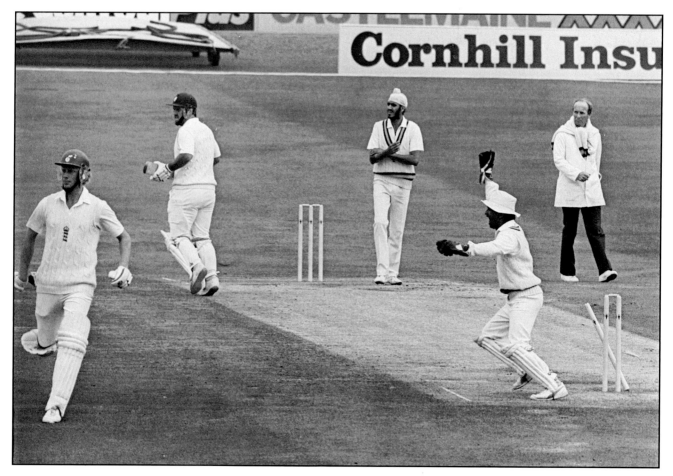

No wonder the Indians looked happy but really they must have expected sterner opposition than this. Vengsarkar, in pride of place here, had the match of his dreams, but everyone chipped in and the only disappointment was that the match finished so early on the fourth day.

Third Test

EDGBASTON · 3–8 July

England, but for a tiresome interruption of almost an hour for bad light on the last day, might have won this match. Equally, they could just about have lost it. Needing to make 236 to win, India had collapsed from 58 for no wicket to 101 for 5. More was then dropped at silly point before he had scored, a modest catch which would have given Edmonds five wickets for very few runs and put India in an awkward spot. Azharuddin and More, after the rain, saw India safely through, putting on 69 together.

From England's point of view it could at least be said that the sequence of seven defeats in a row had been halted. Although the series had already been settled and the weather, after the only hot fortnight of the summer, broke on the second day, this was always interesting, even cricket.

It could hardly have opened more dramatically, for England, having won the toss, were soon 0 for 2, Gooch and Athey out, both of them caught behind the wicket off outswingers from Kapil Dev. Gower was in better touch than at Lord's, but both Benson and he had gone before the 100 was up.

Gatting was perilously close to being caught at slip at the very start of his innings, but once settled, treated the Indian bowlers in the dismissive way he does most county attacks. At the end of a rehabilitating day, he was 141 not out. Pringle, having helped him to add 96 for the fifth wicket, assumed some of his captain's belligerent colouring in the process.

England were all out for 390, a total India exactly equalled in dashing style. Almost everyone got runs, and from Gavaskar and Srikkanth downwards they made them quickly. Gatting preferred his three seam bowlers to his spinners for surprisingly long periods, Foster, Radford and Pringle getting through 95 overs as against 42 from Edmonds and Emburey.

England made a better start to their second innings but 150 for 2 was turned into a dismal 235 all out, mainly through the lively Sharma who removed Gooch, Gower and Gatting when each had been in the best part of an hour.

On the last day the spinners had a pitch to work on, but while Edmonds had a long and profitable bowl, Emburey was only allowed seven overs. After a magisterial 54 by Gavaskar, India lost four wickets for 4 runs.

ENGLAND v. INDIA—Third Test

Toss: England

ENGLAND: First Innings

G. A. Gooch, c More, b Kapil Dev	0
M. R. Benson, b Maninder	21
C. W. J. Athey, c. More, b Kapil Dev	0
D. I. Gower, lbw b Sharma	49
*M. W. Gatting, not out	183
D. R. Pringle, c Amarnath, b Shastri	44
J. E. Emburey, c Shastri, b Maninder	38
N. A. Foster, b Binny	17
P. H. Edmonds, b Sharma	18
*B. N. French, b Sharma	8
N. V. Radford, c Gavaskar, b Sharma	0
Extras (lb 7, nb 5)	12
TOTAL	**390**

Fall of Wickets: 1-0, 2-0, 3-61, 4-88, 5-184, 6-278, 7-327, 8-367, 9-384.

Bowling: Kapil Dev 31-6-89-2; Binny 17-1-53-1; Sharma 29.3-2-130-4; Maninder 25-3-66-2; Shastri 14-1-45-1.

ENGLAND: Second Innings

G. A. Gooch, lbw b Sharma	40
M R. Benson, b Shastri	30
C. W. J Athey, c More, b Sharma	38
D. I. Gower, c Gavaskar, b Sharma	26
*M. W. Gatting, lbw b Sharma	26
D. R. Pringle, c More, b Maninder	7
J. E. Emburey, not out	27
N. A. Foster, run out	0
P. H. Edmonds, c Binny, b Maninder	10
†B. N. French, c More, b Sharma	1
N. V. Radford, c Azharuddin, b Sharma	1
Extras (lb 6, b 10, w 2, nb 11)	29
TOTAL	**235**

Fall of Wickets: 1-49, 2-102, 3-152, 4-163, 5-190, 6-190, 7-190, 8-217, 9-229.

Bowling: Kapil Dev 7-1-38-0; Binny 16-1-41-0; Sharma 22-4-56-6; Amarnath 2-1-2-0; Maninder 22-5-41-2; Shastri 23-8-39-1.

INDIA: First Innings

S. M. Gavaskar, b Pringle	29
K. Srikkanth, c Pringle, b Radford	23
M. Amarnath, b Edmonds	79
D. B. Vengsarkar, c Gooch, b Radford	38
M. Azharuddin, c French, b Foster	64
R. J. Shastri, c Gooch, b Foster	18
*Kapil Dev, c French, b Foster	26
†K. S. More, c French, b Emburey	48
R. M. H. Binny, c Gower, b Emburey	40
C. Sharma, c Gower, b Pringle	9
Maninder Singh, not out	0
Extras (lb 7, b 3, w 1, nb 5)	15
TOTAL	**390**

Fall of Wickets: 1-53, 2-58, 3-139, 4-228, 5-266, 6-275, 7-302, 8-370, 9-385.

Bowling: Radford 35-3-131-2; Foster 41-9-93-3; Pringle 21-2-61-2; Edmonds 24-7-55-1; Emburey 18.5-7-40-2.

INDIA: Second Innings

S. M. Gavaskar, c French, b Foster	54
K. Srikkanth, c Pringle, b Edmonds	23
M. Amarnath, c French, b Edmonds	16
D. B. Vengsarkar, c French, b Edmonds	0
M. Azharuddin, not out	29
R. J. Shastri, c Emburey, b Edmonds	0
†K. S. More, not out	31
Extras (lb 15, b 1, w 1, nb 4)	21
TOTAL (5 wkts)	**174**

Fall of Wickets: 1-58, 2-101, 3-101, 4-104, 5-105.

Bowling: Foster 22-9-48-1; Radford 3-0-17-0; Pringle 16-5-33-0; Edmonds 28-11-31-4; Emburey 7-1-19-0; Gatting 2-0-10-0.

Umpires: H. D. Bird and B. J. Meyer

Match drawn.

Gooch goes for a duck, Srikkanth takes off, and Benson, displacing Slack, shows what little expression helmet and visor allow. This was Gooch's third Test innings of single figures in succession.

LEFT Shastri may well look up wonderingly but Gatting has come down the pitch and hit him straight for 6, as he also did to Maninder.

RIGHT However vulnerable Gatting may be to the ball cutting back at him, when he drives to the off everything is usually right: head still, weight disposed, follow-through classically straight.

BELOW Edmonds seems less happy but he enjoyed himself for nearly an hour before the bustling Sharma hit his stumps.

Foster bowled 26 overs on the second day, not only getting late movement off the seam but occasionally warming the batsman up. Vengsarkar, left, knew at what and what not to play but Azharuddin, right, who had a poor match at Headingley, got the odd one in the ribs, a more likely consequence for one of his method on a pitch of uneven bounce.

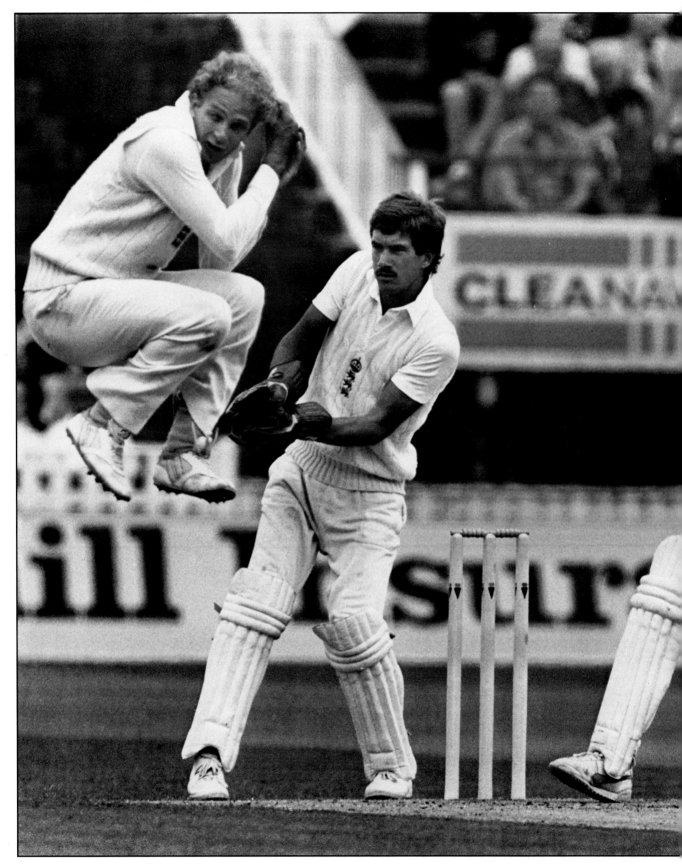

LEFT Gower has had much opportunity for practice in vertical take-off over recent years and it was scarcely surprising he needed a rest before the end of the season. Azharuddin was severe on any variations in length during his three hours on view.

BELOW Amarnath, unfit at Headingley, returned to make top score of 79. A year younger than Gavaskar he has, at 36, had more violent ups and downs than most Test cricketers. If his bowling has grown increasingly amiable, his batting showed both at Lord's and here that his technique is as sound as ever.

LEFT AND ABOVE Kapil Dev's innings were mostly brief and to the point. He wasted no time here but after hitting five resounding boundaries, skied Foster to cloud-height. French, having to make plenty of ground, safely held it.

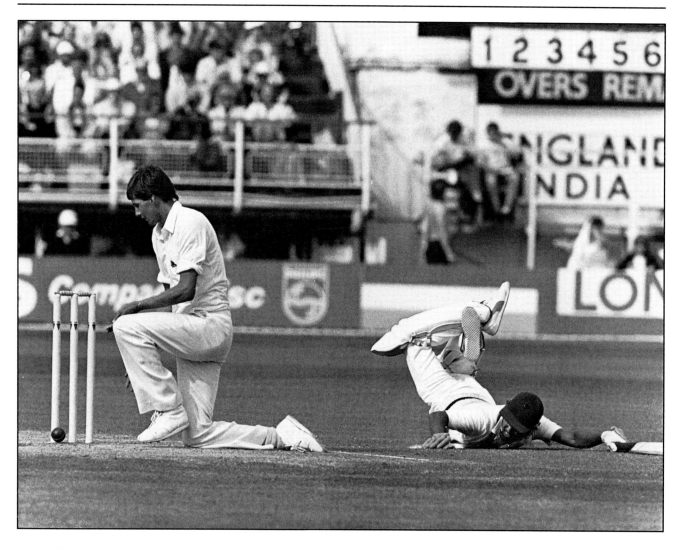

ABOVE More is more likely to be flat on his face keeping wicket than batting but here he has to fling himself full length. Foster, as it happened, failed to gather the ball.

RIGHT Not a mirror image nor one writ in water but a rare example of companionship. Especially for England, for whom such a score was something of a mirage.

LEFT Pringle, usually more dopey than aggressive in expression, seems to mean business here but wherever the batsmen were they got home all right.

ABOVE Foster may not have run
More out on the previous page
but here More has run him out.
Possibly Foster got a bar in the
way. Gavaskar either received a
bail in the eye or ingested some
foreign substance.

RIGHT More has caught Pringle
off Maninder and a few minutes
later he took another catch, his
fifth of the match, this time off
Sharma.

LEFT Gooch departs, lbw to
Sharma who took 6 for 58 and 10
for 188 in the match.

India were soon well on their way to a 3–0 sweep but Edmonds, in a fine spell, halted them in their tracks. Shastri is taken here at slip by Emburey for 0. Gooch, who often likes to keep the batsman in suspense, had first passed the ball on.

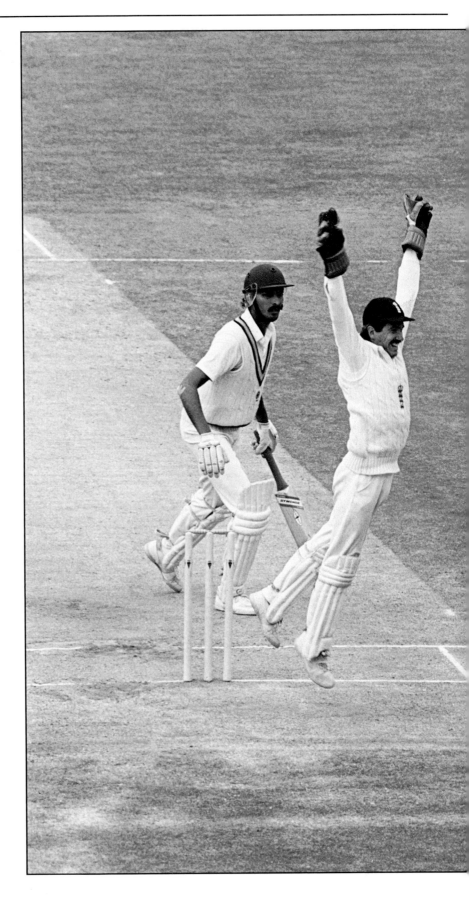

LEFT More, coming in at 105 for 5, immediately prods the ball at Athey who fails to hold it. Edmonds looks gleeful; possibly he has seen the stroke but not its consequence.

ABOVE RIGHT A drawn match but no doubt about the winners of the Cornhill Trophy. Indians in England need something to cheer and their team handsomely provided it. No one could possibly have grudged their success or doubted their superiority over the three matches.

BELOW RIGHT Chetan Sharma, holding trophy, had on the day more to celebrate than anyone.

First Test

LORD'S · July 24–29

There was a moment on the fourth day when England seemed to have jumped out of the frying pan into the fire. That is to say, having been scorched at Lord's by India, it looked as if, in a match following a similar pattern, they were going to suffer equally at the hands of New Zealand. 35 behind on the first innings England, with a long and fragile tail, lost four wickets for 136 in their second. Bad light and Gooch in turn prevented a distressing repetition of events.

England, winning the toss for a change on a decent day, batted more convincingly than of late, though 235 for 4 declined to 307 all out. Hadlee, bowling beautifully in short, sharp spells, soon sent Gooch packing but the batting of Moxon and Athey, sideways on and with the left arm doing the work, pleased the purists. Unfortunately, before the series was over, their correctness of technique was offset by their fallibility, especially against Hadlee.

Gower, looking at first as if Hadlee might get him with any ball, later batted near to his unruffled best. Willey, replacing Emburey who was nursing a broken nose, saw to it that the second half of the innings was not again total misery.

New Zealand, having lost Wright and Rutherford to Dilley, each for 0, were put into a happier frame by Edgar and Martin Crowe, who added 210 together. A score of at least 450 looked on the cards when both were out within the space of three runs. Crowe, after a free and faultless innings of 106, gave a surprised Edmonds a gentle return catch. Only Coney of the remainder looked comfortable against the persistent Edmonds, who took 4 for 97 in 42 overs.

Gray, the New Zealand left arm spinner, turned out more of a problem on the last two days than Hadlee. He bowled 46 overs and took the wickets of Athey, Gower and Gatting, using the rough to some purpose. Gooch remained unperturbed, if only towards the end of a long and sober innings exactly fluent. He batted for over seven hours and hit twenty-two boundaries in his 183, his seventh Test hundred. Willey, for the second time in the match, shored up the ruins.

ENGLAND v. NEW ZEALAND — First Test

Toss: England

ENGLAND: First Innings

G. A. Gooch, c Smith, b Hadlee	18
M. D. Moxon, lbw b Hadlee	74
C. W. J. Athey, c J. J. Crowe, b Hadlee	44
D. I. Gower, c M. D. Crowe, b Bracewell	62
*M. W. Gatting, b Hadlee	2
P. Willey, lbw b Watson	44
P. H. Edmonds, c M. D. Crowe, b Hadlee	6
†B. N. French, retired hurt	0
G. R. Dilley, c Smith, b Hadlee	17
N. A. Foster, b Watson	8
N. V. Radford, not out	12
Extras (lb 7, b 6, nb 7)	20
TOTAL	307

Fall of Wickets: 1-27, 2-102, 3-196, 4-198, 5-237, 6-258, 7-271, 8-285, 9-307.

Bowling: Hadlee 37.5-11-80-6; Watson 30-7-70-2; M. D. Crowe 8-1-38-0; Coney 4-0-12-0; Bracewell 26-8-65-1; Gray 13-9-29-0.

ENGLAND: Second Innings

G. A. Gooch, c Watson, b Bracewell	183
M. D. Moxon, lbw b Hadlee	5
C. W. J. Athey, b Gray	16
D. I. Gower, b Gray	3
*M. W. Gatting, c M. D. Crowe, b Gray	26
P. Willey, b Bracewell	42
P. H. Edmonds, not out	9
Extras (lb 6, w 1, nb 4)	11
TOTAL (6 wickets dec.)	295

Fall of Wickets: 1-9, 2-68, 3-72, 4-136, 5-262, 6-295.

Bowling: Hadlee 27-3-78-1; Watson 17-2-50-0; Gray 46-14-83-3; M. D. Crowe 4-0-13-0; Bracewell 23.4-7-57-2; Rutherford 3-0-8-0.

NEW ZEALAND: First Innings

J. G. Wright, b Dilley	0
B. A. Edgar, c Gatting, b Gooch	83
K. R. Rutherford, c Gooch, b Dilley	0
M. D. Crowe, c and b Edmonds	106
J. J. Crowe, c Gatting, b Edmonds	18
*J. V. Coney, c Gooch, b Radford	51
E. J. Gray, c Gower, b Edmonds	11
R. J. Hadlee, b Edmonds	19
†I. D. S. Smith, c Edmonds, b Dilley	18
J. G. Bracewell, not out	1
W. Watson, lbw b Dilley	1
Extras (lb 9, b 4, w 6, nb 15)	34
TOTAL	342

Fall of Wickets: 1-2, 2-5, 3-215, 4-218, 5-274, 6-292, 7-310, 8-340, 9-340.

Bowling: Dilley 35.1-9-82-4; Foster 25-6-56-0; Radford 25-4-71-1; Edmonds 42-10-97-4; Gooch 13-6-23-1.

NEW ZEALAND: Second Innings

B. A. Edgar, c. Gower, b Foster	0
J. G Wright, c Gower, b Dilley	0
K. R. Rutherford, not out	24
M. D. Crowe, not out	11
Extras (lb 4, nb 2)	6
TOTAL (2 wickets)	41

Fall of Wickets: 1-0, 2-8.

Bowling: Foster 3-1-13-1; Dilley 6-3-5-1; Edmonds 5-0-18-0; Gower 1-0-1-0.

Umpires: H. D. Bird and A. G. T. Whitehead.

Match drawn.

England are out for 307 and Hadlee, with his loping vulpine run, has bowled 37.5 overs to take 6 for 80. There can never have been a better example of the fast bowler's craft, irrespective of result. Cunning, patience, accuracy, intelligence, variety were all on display, the approach a model of economy, the action classical.

LEFT AND RIGHT Athey and Moxon batted for 92 minutes and 246 minutes respectively, much in the manner of Yorkshiremen of the old school. As orthodox and as pale as Hutton, they stirred old memories before Hadlee did for them both. Athey was always going the quicker, eager to get on with it, and he looked set for great things when he edged Hadlee to slip. Moxon missed nothing on the leg stump but, like Gatting a few minutes later, failed to cope with a ball that whipped back at him.

RIGHT This was more like the Gower of 1985; no helmet, no worries, the ball thudding against the boards with not a soul moving.

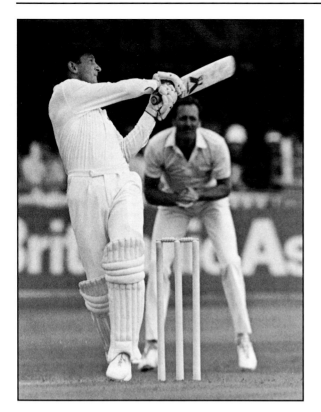

Not the start of a race, or flight from a male streaker, but the end of Edmond's innings, c M. Crowe b Hadlee 6. Edmonds had struggled for 45 minutes with not much to show for it.

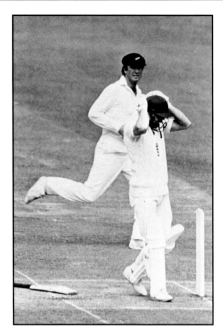

Not a particularly friendly ball for Hadlee to produce for his inexperienced county colleague and it caught French unawares. Slow to pick it up, he turned and was struck on the back of the helmet. Confused and bleeding he was attended to eventually and carted off for stitching. Athey, a competent substitute, took his place but Coney indulgently agreed to let old stager Taylor, a chance presence on the ground, return to the boards. Bobby Parks in due course replaced him and no doubt Parks's father and Godfrey Evans were by now in the wings awaiting a summons. It will be Max Miller next.

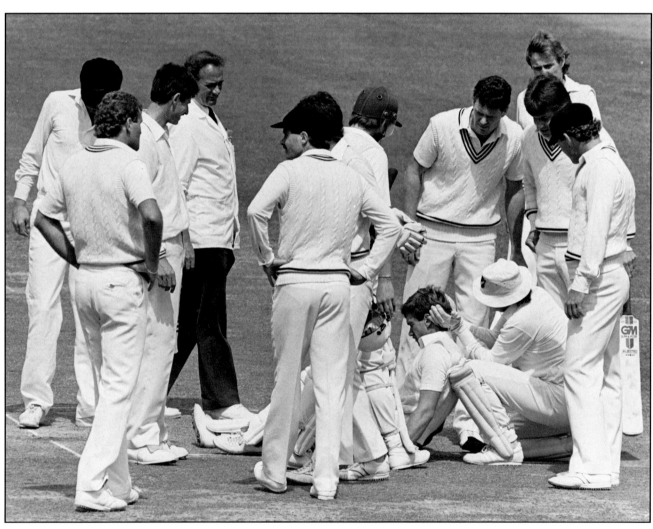

Martin Crowe batted for the best part of six hours, scarcely making a hurried or crude movement. He brings the same sort of assurance and weight to batting as Dennis Amiss in his prime. His 106 contained eleven boundaries, hit on both sides of the wicket off the meat of the bat. In defence he is meticulously correct, head obtrusively over the ball, and one of the best on-drivers in the game.

LEFT Bruce Edgar batted 18 minutes longer than Crowe for 23 less runs, a disparity less than one might have thought. Stolid and adhesive in the early stages, Edgar, once warmed up, showed that he had a stroke or two up his sleeve.

RIGHT Jeremy Coney was never easy to shift. He made 51 good runs here, harsh on anything short. If he appears too physically restless ever to look a composed batsman, he is a well-enough organised one.

BELOW The old trouper trots off, after a neat soft shoe shuffle, and Bobby Parks becomes the third understudy for the wounded French. Both Parks's father and grandfather took part in a Test at Lord's but this was not quite the same thing.

BELOW Moxon in his first innings was going well when Hadlee, in his second spell, brought one back down the hill to get him lbw. Here, in the second innings, he has him lbw again for only 5. Hadlee's reverse position screech at the umpire when he appeals seems curiously at odds with his generally unassuming demeanour.

RIGHT Evan Gray had a good match, batting for an hour, and then removing Athey, Gower and Gatting for not many in England's second innings.

Gooch had long since made the
match safe and was approaching
his double century when he lifted
Bracewell to Watson just in from
the pavilion fence.

RIGHT Willey made 44 and 42 in the match and justified his presence as replacement for Emburey, although he did not bowl. His square leg-facing stance is an absurdity but seems improbably not to interfere with the correct placement of the feet when playing to the off.

BELOW New Zealand had only a token hour's batting at the end but it was long enough for both Wright and Edgar to be out for ducks, Wright getting a pair. Gower caught them both, in this picture Wright off Dilley at third slip.

Second Test

TRENT BRIDGE · August 7–12

Although in the end they had, because of the weather, only a few overs to spare New Zealand eventually outplayed England and won comfortably by 8 wickets. Hadlee took ten wickets in the match, setting England up in each innings, and then he, Gray and Bracewell batted so coolly that a score of 144 for 5 was turned into a total of 413. Starting their second innings 157 behind England were at one stage 104 for 6. Emburey, by methods of his own devising, which rarely involve getting into line behind anything quick, contributed a valiant 75, his highest Test score, and the last four wickets produced 126.

New Zealand, needing only 74 to win, lost two wickets for 19. If there were momentary visions of last-ditch excitement, Martin Crowe and Jeremy Coney rapidly dispelled them.

The length and strength of New Zealand's batting and the innocuousness of England's bowling left New Zealand with all the cards. All the same, had England batted at all reasonably in their second innings they could, and should, have saved the match. Gooch, Gower, Athey and Gatting fell to the spin of Bracewell and Gray who both made the occasional ball turn and bounce. But considering that not much more than an hour's play was possible on the fourth day, it only needed a decent innings from a recognised batsman for New Zealand to run out of time. It would have been an injustice and it was not forthcoming.

Bracewell had a tremendous match, scoring his first Test hundred and taking three valuable wickets in England's second innings. Gray, too, in more plodding fashion added a useful 50 to effective bowling.

England, during New Zealand's long innings, looked as dilatory and devoid of ideas as they had ever done under Willis and Gower on their bad days.

ENGLAND v. NEW ZEALAND — Second Test

Toss: New Zealand

ENGLAND: First Innings

G. A. Gooch, lbw b Hadlee	18
M. D. Moxon, b Hadlee	9
C. W. J. Athey, lbw b Watson	55
D. I. Gower, lbw b Gray	71
*M. W. Gatting, b Hadlee	17
D. R. Pringle, c Watson, b Stirling	21
J. E. Emburey, c Smith, b Hadlee	8
P. H. Edmonds, c Smith, b Hadlee	0
J. G. Thomas, b Hadlee	28
†B. N. French, c Coney, b Watson	21
G. C. Small, not out	2
Extras (lb 3, b 1, nb 2)	6
TOTAL	256

Fall of Wickets: 1-18, 2-43, 3-126, 4-170, 5-176, 6-191, 7-191, 8-205, 9-240.

Bowling: Hadlee 32-7-80-6; Stirling 17-3-62-1; Gray 13-4-30-1; Watson 16.5-6-51-2; Coney 7-1-18-0; Bracewell 4-1-11-0.

ENGLAND: Second Innings

G. A. Gooch, c Coney, b Bracewell	17
M. D. Moxon, c Smith, b Hadlee	23
P. H. Edmonds, lbw b Hadlee	20
C. W. J. Athey, c Smith, b Bracewell	6
D. I. Gower, c J. J. Crowe, b Bracewell	26
*M. W. Gatting, c Smith, b Gray	4
D. R. Pringle, c Gray, b Stirling	9
J. E. Emburey, c M. D. Crowe, b Hadlee	75
J. G. Thomas, c Gray, b Stirling	10
†B. N. French, not out	12
G. C. Small lbw b Hadlee	12
Extras (lb 9, b 4, w1, nb 2)	16
TOTAL	230

Fall of Wickets: 1-23, 2-47, 3-63, 4-87, 5-98, 6-104, 7-178, 8-203, 9-203.

Bowling: Hadlee 33.1-15-60-4; Stirling 18-5-48-2; Bracewell 11-5-29-3; Watson 9-3-25-0; Gray 24-9-55-1.

NEW ZEALAND: First Innings

J. G. Wright, c Athey, b Small	58
B. A. Edgar, lbw b Thomas	8
J. J. Crowe, c French, b Small	23
M. D. Crowe, c Edmonds, b Emburey	28
*J. V. Coney run out	24
E. J. Gray, c Athey, b Edmonds	50
R. J. Hadlee, c Gooch, b Thomas	68
J. G. Bracewell, c. Moxon, b Emburey	110
†I. D. S. Smith, lbw b Edmonds	2
D. A. Stirling, b Small	26
W. Watson, not out	8
Extras (lb 4, w 2, nb 2)	8
TOTAL	413

Fall of Wickets: 1-39, 2-85, 3-92, 4-142, 5-144, 6-239, 7-318, 8-326, 9-391.

Bowling: Small 38-12-88-3; Thomas 39-5-124-2; Pringle 20-1-58-0, Edmonds 28-11-52-2; Emburey 42.5-17-87-2; Gooch 2-2-0-0.

NEW ZEALAND: Second Innings

J. G. Wright, b Emburey	7
J. J. Crowe, lbw b Small	2
M. D. Crowe, not out	48
*J. V. Coney, not out	20
TOTAL (2 wickets)	77

Fall of Wickets: 1-5, 2-19.

Bowling: Small 8-3-10-1; Thomas 4-0-16-0; Emburey 6-1-15-1; Edmonds 4-1-16-0; Pringle 2-0-16-0; Gower 0-0-4-0 (1 nb).

Umpires D. J. Constant and K. E. Palmer.

NEW ZEALAND won by 8 wickets

England's selectors – Alan Smith, Fred Titmus, Peter May and Philip Sharpe, together with Mickey Stewart, the Assistant Manager for the winter tour of Australia – have a look at the pitch. Little do they know what is in store. The briefcases suggest a wealth of information but perhaps they only contain sandwiches.

LEFT Moxon, comfortable though he looked in his innings of 74 at Lord's, subsequently lost his way against Hadlee and eventually his place. Hadlee removed him four times in four innings, bowling him here for 9 and getting him caught off his outswinger in the second innings for 23.

BELOW Gatting had some nasty moments at Lord's against Hadlee even before he was bowled for 2. He needed and must desperately have wanted runs here but he had got no further than 17 when Hadlee bowled him again.

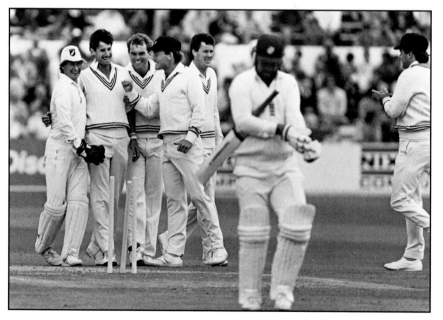

RIGHT Umpire Constant has not joined the PLO but England's batting and the English climate might make it tempting. Gower, left, was eventually lbw to Gray, right, for 71, not the first time that Gray took Gower's wicket.

Martin Crowe mourns the loss of his captain, run out for 24 just when New Zealand were getting on top. It was scarcely Crowe's fault, for Coney, slow to respond to his call, failed only by inches to get home.

LEFT Small made an encouraging
start, taking two wickets in quick
succession. Wright was
threatening dire revenge for his
pair at Lord's when he was caught
at square leg, and Crowe, seven
runs later, was well held by
French diving to his right.

BELOW When Hadlee arrived, New
Zealand were 144–5 and had lost
the advantage he had gained
them the day before. By the close
New Zealand were 211 for 5,
Hadlee 53 not out. Twenty-four
had come from boundaries, mostly
slashed through the covers off the
quicker bowlers.

If it wasn't for the scoreboard you might think Hadlee had been listening to a racing commentary and a certainty had just gone down. But John Bracewell doesn't score a Test hundred every day – in fact he had never scored one – and at the other end Watson can scarcely have expected to bear such a responsibility. However, all was well, Bracewell got his hundred, Watson carried his bat, and everyone could go home happy.

John Bracewell had the year of his life. Last winter he failed to make the side to Australia but, flown out in mid series, hit 83 not out in the second Test at Sydney and took five wickets. At Auckland a few weeks later he mopped up Australia, taking ten wickets. Before this series began his Test batting average was 16 and his Sydney innings was his only score of over fifty. You would not have thought it watching him bat here.

LEFT Things were looking desperate for England with Stirling adding 65 with Bracewell for the ninth wicket. Small, however, whipped out Stirling's off stump when he had made 26. The crowd took to Small who, off a shortish run, was the only one of England's quicker bowlers to do himself any good.

ABOVE Moxon goes yet again to Hadlee, gathered into the wicket-keeper's stomach, and England are 47 for 2, over 100 runs behind.

BELOW Not a seance, or magic tricks by the umpires, but another boring meter reading. Soon they would all be in the pavilion, reading newspapers.

LEFT Gatting, having survived
another torrid spell from Hadlee
by the skin of his teeth, was out to
the first ball from Gray, beaten by
the turn and clutched in by the
wicket-keeper. Gatting's four
innings of the series so far
produced 49 runs.

BELOW Gower had seemed in no
great trouble but Bracewell got
this one to turn and lift as soon as
he came on for Hadlee. Jeff Crowe
caught him at slip and England
were 104 for 6.

ABOVE LEFT Emburey, one might have imagined, would have played second fiddle to Pringle in their seventh wicket partnership of 74, but in fact Pringle contributed only 9. Emburey steered, paddled and scooped until Hadlee put a stop to it.

BELOW LEFT Small has gallantly helped French to put on 27 for the last wicket, both of them laying about with a will. Sadly, then, he offered no stroke at Hadlee and was lbw. New Zealand needed only 74 to win.

ABOVE RIGHT Emburey took a quick wicket, Small took another, but Martin Crowe put the full face of the bat to the ball. Thomas and Edmonds were each struck for 16 in 4 overs, Pringle for 16 in two. Small took 1 for 10 in 8 overs which would have been handy in a one-day match but not good enough here.

BELOW RIGHT Coney and Gatting shake on it and New Zealand have won only their second Test in England, their fourth in the sixty-two matches between the two countries. Gatting would have plenty to make up for at the Oval. For Coney, all he needed to do was to hang on.

Third Test

THE OVAL · August 21–26

To salvage anything from a depressing summer, England needed to win at the Oval. For New Zealand a draw was all they required to win their first ever series in England. The weather, which hampered New Zealand at Lord's, was this time on their side.

There is no knowing that New Zealand would have lost this match, even had a full day's play been possible throughout. But there was only just over an hour's play after the week-end and by Monday morning England had built up a lead of 101, with Botham going strong and five wickets in hand.

For the only time in the six Tests England were not behind on the first innings. New Zealand, put in to bat on a cloudy, threatening day, were bowled out on the third morning, after many interruptions, for 287. Botham, recalled to the side, took three of the first four wickets and Dilley most of the remainder.

When England began their innings on the Saturday, time was already running out. But after Athey, Gooch and Lamb had gone for 62, Gower and Gatting, in the most refreshing English batting of the year, took the score to 281 without being parted. This was Gower at his serene best, persuading and leaning on the ball, charming it through the covers and off his legs. Gatting, as if entranced, watched for a while and then pounced. He was vigilant against Hadlee and ruthless towards everyone else. They ran splendidly between the wickets and their styles and methods were a nice contrast.

New Zealand, on the first day, could have been in worse trouble than they were. Had Edmonds, who fielded brilliantly all summer, not dropped a sitter at mid-off soon after Gray had come in, New Zealand would have been 115 for 5. He must have been calculating his wife's royalties.

ENGLAND v. NEW ZEALAND—Third Test

Toss: England

NEW ZEALAND: First Innings

J. G. Wright, b Edmonds	119
B. A. Edgar, c Gooch, b Botham	1
J. J. Crowe, lbw b Botham	8
M. D. Crowe, lbw b Dilley	13
*J. V. Coney, c Gooch, b Botham	38
E. J. Gray, b Dilley	30
R. J. Hadlee, c French, b Edmonds	6
J. G. Bracewell, c Athey, b Emburey	3
†T. E. Blain, c Gooch, b Dilley	37
D. A. Stirling, not out	18
E. J. Chatfield, c. French, b Dilley	5
Extras (b 1, w 1, nb 7)	9

TOTAL 287

Fall of Wickets: 1-17, 2-31, 3-59, 4-106, 5-175, 6-192, 7-197, 8-251, 9-280.

Bowling: Dilley 28.2-4-92-4; Small 18-5-36-0; Botham 25-4-75-3; Emburey 31-15-39-1; Edmonds 22-10-29-2; Gooch 4-1-15-0.

NEW ZEALAND: Second Innings

J. G. Wright, not out	7
B. A. Edgar, not out	0

TOTAL (0 wicket) 7

Bowling: Botham 1-0-7-0.

ENGLAND: First Innings

G. A. Gooch, c Sterling, b Hadlee	32
C. W. J. Athey, lbw b Hadlee	17
D. I. Gower, b Chatfield	131
A. J. Lamb, b Chatfield	0
*M. W. Gatting, b Chatfield	121
I. T. Botham, not out	59
J. E. Emburey, not out	9
Extras (lb 9, w 5, nb 5)	19

TOTAL (5 wickets dec.) 388

To bat: †B. N. French, P. H. Edmonds, G. R. Dilley, G. C. Small.

Fall of Wickets: 1-38, 2-62, 3-62, 4-285, 5-326.

Bowling: Hadlee 23.5-6-92-2; Sterling 9-0-71-0; Chatfield 21-7-73-3; Gray 21-4-74-0; Bracewell 11-1-51-0; Coney 5-0-18-0.

Umpires: H. D. Bird and D. R. Shepherd.

Match drawn.

Botham removed the hypnotised Edgar with his first ball, steered obligingly to Gooch at second slip, above, and in his next over Jeff Crowe, almost caught at third slip first ball, was lbw. Coney, in Botham's second spell, was next to go, falling for the sucker long hop and mishooking. Gooch below, took the catch at second slip.

Nobody seems in much doubt about Crowe's fate, right, although umpire Shepherd has yet to make a move. His hands may have been cold. At the end of the day Botham had taken 3 for 36, in the process overtaking Lillee and becoming the leading Test wicket-taker.

ABOVE John Wright, after a distressing season, finally came good, making 119 out of 287. He looks anxious here, for Botham has failed to cling on to a sharp chance. But, off his legs especially, Wright was solid as a rock and productive.

LEFT Gray as usual sold his wicket dearly, putting on 69 with Wright. Dilley finally flattened his off stump and New Zealand were 175 for 5.

RIGHT 'We're just a couple of swells'. Maybe, but also thoroughly suspicious, as if someone was going through their pockets in the dressing room. Wright at last was out, but Stirling and Blain were going strong. Perhaps it was time for a cup of tea.

LEFT Athey needed a decent innings here. He began confidently but when he was 17 Hadlee beat him and Shepherd got his finger out.

RIGHT Gooch hooks but Stirling is going to catch him, running in from long leg. So Hadlee has his second wicket and Gooch has played his last Test innings of the year. He batted five times, scored 268 runs (183 in one innings) and averaged 53.

BELOW Gower might have gone when he was 3, but thereafter was sweetness and light. Runs flowed effortlessly, just as they had done a year earlier against Australia. Lamb was out for a duck, bowled Chatfield, but on Saturday evening England were 281 for 3, Gower 129 not out, Gatting 86 not out. This was Gower's only hundred of the summer but the manner of it made up for everything. Together he and Gatting put on 223.

RIGHT For some reason it was too much for Hadlee, who produced three vicious bouncers in a row. The third one surprised Gower who only just got out of the way at the last second, the ball going for four off the splice.

BELOW Gatting, catching Gower's mood, found all his troubles melting away. He sensibly let Gower make the running, himself bringing in the thunder as necessary. There could scarcely have been a greater contrast in method, the one blonde and elegant, the other paunchy and punchy.

Botham was not going to be upstaged, long though he had to wait for his cue. He began gently, contributing only 5 in a stand of 41 with Gatting, but thereafter banged away as only he can.

He mishooked Stirling once, left, Blain circling under an immense skier like a rudderless dinghy, but in Stirling's next over he savaged him for 24, two leg-side sixes and three fours. Roberts had once hit Botham for 24 in an over in Port of Spain, hitherto a Test record. Trust Botham to have it both ways. Rain, unfortunately, was closing in. Botham faced only 32 balls, batting for 48 minutes and making 59 not out.

It was what everyone wanted to see and, brief encounter though it was, few can have felt they did not get their money's worth. Even Hadlee had been suddenly made to seem human, his fielders scattered far and wide.

There was to be no reprieve for England. On Monday there had been one hour's play and on the last day only one over. It was a great disappointment, if not perhaps for the New Zealanders who may have saved themselves sore hands and plenty of running. But they were entitled to their celebration, in a bleak and empty Oval, and in the months to come will be able to savour memories of

their success.

The 1986 New Zealanders were not, as a side, outstandingly gifted, but they had a great bowler in Richard Hadlee and a fine batsman in Martin Crowe.

Most important, they appeared to enjoy each other's company as well as their cricket and to give it just the right degree of importance. No one could wish them other than well.

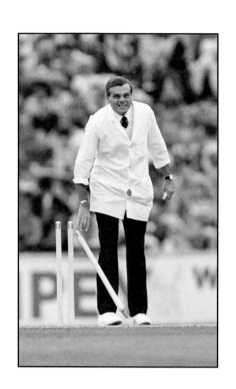